To family and friends

ASK ME A QUESTION

Shristi G

A Marriage Guide's Love Story

Inkfeathers Publishing

www.inkfeathers.com

Copyright © Shristi G, 2023

Ask Me A Question
by Shristi G
Paperback Edition

First Published in 2023 in India by

Inkfeathers Publishing
Vivek Vihar, New Delhi 110095
www.inkfeathers.com

Edited by Vitasha Saraf

ISBN 978-93-90882-93-9

Contents

Author's Note

My hero, Rithik, is drawn from the questions my friends and family had asked their significant others before marriage, while my heroine, Avni, is drawn from the fears and jitters one faces before entering into married life.

Marriage as an institution is a very scary concept. When you are on the verge of getting married, there are a lot of questions running through your mind. It's impossible to find answers to every question, but the answers sometimes help to decide if or not one should marry the significant other. My idea for the book came from family and friends who are married. I asked them about their feelings, emotions, and a general understanding of the institution called marriage. There was one common understanding of marriage. Marriage is a partnership, where you don't necessarily agree with each other, but you always respect each other. You can survive a loveless married life but not a respectless one. I hope that it's an entertaining read for all.

Prologue

'Rithik, you are almost thirty! When are you going to get married?'

'Rithik, if you want, I can find you a suitable bride!'

'Rithik, you are so handsome! You just say the word and I will line up girls in your house.'

'Rithik, how do you treat those patients when you don't even know what married life is?'

Rithik Dhananjay Kashyap had heard it all in the past five years of his career. He was fed up with people constantly telling him to get married. Indian parents really needed to grow out of their obsession with marriage. It was tiring now. He wanted to give a befitting reply to all of them but before he could utter a word, his mother called him out.

He joined his mother, who introduced him to a man named Kadam Karamsheel. Rithik joined his palms and greeted the man.

'He is your father's friend,' explained Kusum Kashyap, his mother. Suddenly, they were joined by a very timid girl. She whispered something in the ears of Kadam Karamsheel and walked away. It was odd. The girl almost had a frightened look on her face.

Who was she?

He thought and in came the reply, 'That is my daughter, Avni. She is very shy and rarely talks. We are looking for a groom for her,' said Kadam Karamsheel, eyeing Rithik as if he read Rithik's mind.

Rithik wanted to tell Mr Karamsheel that he wasn't looking for a bride but a gentle nudge from his mother stopped him. After not getting a response from the Kashyaps, Mr Karamsheel excused himself and walked towards the direction where his daughter had earlier gone.

'Ma, you know I don't like this. Why did you stop me from correcting him?' asked an angry Rithik.

'Rithik, sometimes we need to maintain the dignity of the place. This is someone's wedding day and place. I don't think you would want to cause a scene here,' remarked Kusum.

Rithik knew his mother was right but still, it bothered him that people couldn't mind their own business. He nodded and asked his mother, 'Are we leaving any time soon?'

Rithik mentally patted his father for successfully escaping this event. He feigned an ankle injury earlier and was now resting at home. While Rithik was playing the designated driver and companion to his mother at this wedding.

'Come on, let's go in,' urged Kusum to her son.

After leaving his mom in the hall where the functions were taking place, Rithik excused himself and went in search of some quiet place. He finally found some peace outside, on the balcony of the third floor. The moon was shining brightly but then something else caught his attention. It was the girl, Mr Karamsheel's daughter, Avni.

*****

Avni had also walked onto the balcony seeking some peace and solace. She was tired of her relatives. She needed a break before she went back in for the second dose of nagging.

'It's beautiful, isn't it?' came a voice behind her. 'The moon,' the voice prompted.

Avni didn't say anything.

'Oh! You are the silent type. I like those kinds of people. The observant one. It has been said that they have the loudest minds. So, I am honoured to be in your presence,' said the stranger.

The stranger was making Avni curious with his words. She wanted to turn towards him, see him, talk to him, but she merely bobbed her head.

'Have you seen Avni?' Avni knew that voice that came from a distance. It was her mother asking for her. She had to go before her mother came out and found her with this stranger. Her mother would then cook up a story in her mind that would lead to more nagging and questions, taking away all the little peace remaining in her life.

With that thought in mind, Avni ran back inside from the balcony, hoping that the stranger hadn't followed her.

*****

Rithik wanted to run after her, but the fearful look in her eyes stopped him.

What was she so afraid of?

Was it her parents?

Were her parents abusive?

He had so many questions in mind that he wanted the answers to. So, he decided that he would ask his mother more about Avni and made his way down towards the hall where his mother was.

'Ma, it's getting late,' Rithik tried to reason out with his mother. Kusum nodded and followed her son towards the car after bidding farewell to the hosts.

Once in the car, Rithik asked his mother, 'Tell me about Avni.'

'Avni?' His mother had narrowed brows.

'Ma, you know whom I am talking about,' Rithik said, rolling his eyes.

Kusum shrugged and replied, 'I don't know much about her. Your father might help.'

Rithik drove on towards their home. He was curious about Avni, but he couldn't understand the reason.

But why am I curious?

Was it her frightened look?

Rithik's odd interest in the girl wasn't new to him. He was a therapist, after all. Wanting to know the problems that a human is going through was his nature.

*****

Avni was finally back in her bed after a tiring day. She was exhausted and cranky. She wished she could have skipped this function like her male cousins. Wish! If only Avni got whatever she wished for. Twenty-five-year-old Avni had long ago realised that she would probably never get what she wished for, but she had made peace with this. Yet, she was a mere human, bound to be tempted.

The next morning, Avni got a message from her best friend to come by her house. After taking her parents' permission, Avni made her way to her best friend, Tanvi's house.

'Avni!' shrieked Tanvi as soon as she opened the door.

'Tanu, what is wrong? And stop shrieking!' chided Avni.

Tanvi flashed the newspaper in front of her best friend, 'Look!' She said enthusiastically and started reading out loud.

'Prashasti, a famous food blogging page on Instagram is winning the hearts of millions. The page has a fan following of ten million on the social media site. Their social media account introduces them as someone who believes, becomes, and bedazzles. They might have had a slow start but are now conquering the culinary world. Every brand has been offering them contracts to work with them, but they have refused them all. This does make one question their reasons to refuse. No one knows how many people are behind that page. The page that has a fan following of ten million doesn't follow back a single Instagram account, as a result, we have not yet been able to track down the identity of the person behind the page. Nevertheless, we are thankful to the page for its delicious recipes. You will find some of the recipes on the page in our weekly additional magazine.'

With wide eyes, Avni snatched back the newspaper and started reading the article herself. She went on to grab the additional magazine and sure there it was, HER recipes published by the magazine. She was beyond shocked by this.

When Avni, with the help of her best friend, Tanvi, started this page, she had never expected to get ten million followers. But then, as and when her posts grew, so did her followers. And now, she was being featured in a newspaper. This was huge. Avni mentally patted herself for this achievement.

'What are you reading so diligently?' asked Tanvi.

On realising that she was lost in her thoughts with the magazine still in her hand, Avni whispered, 'Nothing,' and kept aside the additional weekly magazine.

An excited Tanvi exclaimed, 'This is not it!'

'It is not?' exclaimed Avni.

Tanvi nodded and grabbed her phone. She then showed Avni the Instagram page that she had been scrolling through before her arrival. The page was managed by both best friends. But it had Avni's name, or more precisely her middle name, Prashasti. After all, they were Avni's recipes. Avni tried to understand what her best friend was trying to tell her by showing her their Instagram page. It had the right name, Prashasti, the blue tick was still there, and the followers... Avni's eyes widened as she saw that they now had twenty million followers. From ten million they had gone on to get twenty million by just being featured in a newspaper. Avni held Tanvi's hands and started a little victory dance. Tanvi joined in as they jumped higher and higher, screaming at the top of their lungs.

After a minute, the best friends plopped down on the sofa with smiles on their faces.

'Avni, I know you don't want to do contracts...' Tanvi grabbed her best friend's hands again... 'But think about it. I know you are afraid that your family won't allow it, but how long are you going to live like this? Don't you want to do something without the constant worry about what if your family finds out? How long will this go on? You are a successful person in your own right, Avni. There are people who look up to you. If not for them, then do this for yourself. Tell your family that you are not the meek little girl they have always told you to be. Tell them that you are bold and beautiful. Tell them that the kitchen they have always sent you to with the hopes to silence you is your centre stage. Tell them that there is life beyond the bars and the boundaries they have always told you to stay behind!' Tanvi said firmly in a breath.

Avni knew that Tanvi was right. But every time she had tried to reason out her accomplishments with her family, they either laughed it off or told her to cook something for them to eat. The first time Avni was told to cook food after being laughed at, she had excitedly gone to the kitchen and baked a cake. But time and again, when her family did the same, Avni finally understood that the kitchen was symbolic of her failure, her failure to find individuality in her family. She was repeatedly sent to the kitchen to be reminded that her life belonged in a bar, within the boundaries. But she still had managed to find a life beyond the kitchen.

Tanvi is right! There is life beyond the boundaries.

And there is nothing to be afraid of.

What's the worst my family could do?

Disown me?

But that would be fine as I am now earning a good amount from my posts on Instagram alone.

If I started doing contracts, then I would earn more.

As Avni was lost deep in her thoughts, she understood what she needed was determination, and then, she would be able to surely achieve the desired result.

With a determined look in her eyes, Avni looked up into her best friend's eyes and said, 'I will think about it!'

A shocked Tanvi stuttered, 'You... you would?'

Chuckling, Avni assured her, 'Yes, I would. You are right, Tanvi. It's about time that I broke the cage to fly and soar up high in the sky!'

Tanvi's eyes glistened with tears. She never expected this day to come so soon. She had been trying to reason out with her best friend for so long. But Avni had never readily agreed to go beyond the limits set by her parents. Now the time had come, and being her best friend, Tanvi would make sure to make it as easy as possible for her best friend.

Avni had never been brave enough to break free from her family, and even right now, she wasn't sure if she would successfully manage to escape. Earlier, Avni wasn't able to break free because she was economically dependent on her family, but now, when she had money and a possibility that more money would flow in, then breaking free seemed like a possibility. She at least had to try it this time.

Avni made her way back home, determination in her steps. But her determined steps faltered when she saw that her parents were setting up her account on matrimonial sites. She stood there numb and watched as her parents went on to describe her as meek, shy, speaks less, and a good cook on the site. She wanted to scream at the unfairness of the situation. She knew this was her chance to speak. But she couldn't. Years of silence told her to stay quiet. But the newfound determination wanted to break free. In the end, the silence won, and Avni didn't tell her parents about her success.

*****

Ever since he had met Avni, Rithik had been restless. It was as if something was pulling him towards her. Even his father couldn't give him more information on Avni. It was surprising that his father didn't know anything about her apart from her name. Rithik stole a glance towards his father. They were seated around the dinner table.

'Dad, it's surprising that you don't know a thing about your friend's daughter,' remarked Rithik.

'Rithik, we were just batchmates. Not exactly the best of buddies,' explained Krishna Kashyap.

Rithik thought that this was a valid explanation. 'But Dad, if you are not exactly friends with Mr Karamsheel, then why did Mom introduce him as one? More importantly, why didn't Mr Karamsheel correct her?'

'That is because Kadam is just like that. He doesn't like to be told that he is wrong. In college, he always tried to befriend me. But you know I stay away from people who have no compassion. Kadam is orthodox in his beliefs. And you know what I have always told you.'

Rithik nodded. 'Change is the only constant and we must adapt to the situation,' he repeated his father's words that he had been hearing since childhood.

Krishna beamed at his son.

Rithik thought about what his father had said. If Mr Karamsheel was orthodox and didn't like to be told that he was wrong, then he could totally understand Avni's frightened look. Suddenly, his chest tugged as he felt something in his heart. He couldn't exactly place what it was. But then his subconscious mind whispered, 'Avni,' and his heart calmed.

Krishna and Kusum Kashyap were not sure why their only son was so curious about Avni Karamsheel. But then, suddenly, something clicked in Kusum's mind, and she gasped.

'Are you fine, Mom?' asked Rithik.

'Yes. Yes,' Kusum smiled, thinking about the possibility.

Yes, it had to be that. She was thinking right. Rithik was interested in Avni. But then she glanced towards her husband. If what her husband had just said was true, then the road ahead would be difficult. But Kusum could make it easy by getting to know Avni. What if she was not like her father? What if she was compassionate? Then, she would make a perfect daughter-in-law. Kusum's eyes gleamed at that possibility. After all, she had been trying to get her son married off. But her son had successfully sent them all off. She was sure that Rithik wouldn't send Avni off. He looked too much interested in her.

That night in her bed, Kusum was mentally planning how she would get in touch with Avni. Now, she knew that she could ask her husband's help. But she wasn't completely sure that her husband would help.

'What are you thinking over there?' Krishna asked, joining her.

'Nothing,' Kusum told him. She felt guilty for lying to him. They had been married for thirty years now. And never had there been a secret among them. But this was about her son. She needed to be quiet about this. Yes, this was for the best. Until she met Avni again, she had to keep all this to herself. Once she was sure that Avni was nothing like her father, only then would she tell the truth to her husband or anyone. But what if she turned out to be exactly like her father? Kusum chided herself for being pessimistic. Her heart told her that Avni was a compassionate woman.

What Does One Ask a Prospective Match?

Dear Rithik,

My parents have started their groom hunt. I know I want an arranged marriage. But I am not sure what I should ask my intended. How would I know that he is the one? I am scared. I don't want to make the wrong decision. Am I wrong in wanting an arranged marriage? Should I tell my parents to stop? Should I keep my mind open to love marriage? Help me! Please!

Thanks in advance!

@aconfusedsoul

Rithik read the message on his Instagram. He re-read it. It was such a simple question. But he needed to be sure before answering her question. He didn't want his answer to be an imposing one. Once he was sure about his answer, he started typing on his phone.

Dear Confused Soul,

First of all, I hope that your parents do find a suitable groom for you. There is nothing wrong with wanting an arranged marriage. As for what you should ask your intended one, then that is all up to you. I could suggest a million questions, but still, there is no guarantee that those questions would be the right ones to base your judgment on. So, I would suggest you think hard. Ask from your confused soul and you might find your question. We are all different, and our priorities are different. So, I cannot completely suggest you any questions. Though, I can give you a few examples. You can ask about what he earns, his beliefs, and his interests. Those are the most basic things that anyone asks their prospective marriage partner.

There is no assurance that your decision will be the right one. You might marry today and end up divorcing the same guy two years later. Marriage is a work in progress. If you cannot accept that, then I don't think you are ready to be married.

Love is not something you go out looking for in the market. There is a total possibility that you might end up loving your husband. However, if you want to fall in love before marriage, then that too should be your choice.

I can only guide you through, not make your decisions. I hope I was helpful.

Dr Rithik D. Kashyap
@yourmarriageguide

Rithik read his reply and then tapped the send button. He tossed his phone aside and made his way to the bathroom to get ready for the day. Being a marriage therapist wasn't an easy task. Nevertheless, he loved his work. It was his parent's marriage that inspired him to choose this field. Rithik's parents had completed thirty years of married life. The rapport between them was endearing. Rithik believed that if his parents' marriage could survive this long then so could anyone else's. It was all about will. But of course, that didn't mean that you needed to survive in an abusive married life. Hence, Rithik chose this profession with the hope to guide people into a successful married life, and also to make people see some sense in an abusive marriage.

Rithik tucked his shirt in, adjusted his tie, grabbed his bags and files, and made his way down to the dining table. Once there, he grabbed a toast and his coffee in the carry mug.

'Those ladies are right. I should start a bride hunt for you. Probably then you would sit and have your breakfast,' chided Kusum.

Rithik gave his mother an appalling look. 'Ma!'

'Don't you "Ma" me. Is it too much to ask to have breakfast in peace, by sitting together, before you leave for the day? Now don't tell me that we all have dinner together every day. It is not enough. Look at yourself. You have started losing weight!'

Rithik looked down at himself. He knew his mother was right. Even he noticed his weight loss. Maybe he should have a proper breakfast and not a rushed one. 'Okay!' he sat down on the chair.

Kusum wasn't sure if she heard it right. 'Did you just…?'

Chuckling, Rithik said, 'Yes, Ma. Come on. Let's have breakfast the proper way,' he smiled at his mother, who was already sitting in front of him with a shocked expression.

'Seema Di, what did you cook this morning?' Rithik called out to their cook.

A confused Seema came out from the kitchen. She hadn't cooked anything new. Like every day, she had prepared toasts for Rithik, and *paranthas* for Kusum Aunty and Krishna Uncle. Before Seema could answer, Kusum picked up a toast and said, 'She has prepared your toast.'

The look his mother was giving him told Rithik that he really needed to eat more and be healthy. He looked over to Seema and requested her, 'Seema Di, would you be kind enough to pack those toasts? I don't want to waste them. I would eat them during the day. Right now, I would have whatever Ma is having.' He smiled at her.

*****

Avni cursed herself for the thousandth time.

Why couldn't I say a word?

She was up in her room while her parents were downstairs planning, mapping, and plotting out her future. They didn't even bother asking her if she wanted what they wanted. Like always, she was expected to follow blindly. She wanted to tell them that enough was enough. She wanted to do so much. But something was pulling her back. On one side, she wanted to break free from her family, but on the other, she didn't want that. She wanted her family to accept her as an individual. She wanted their acknowledgement of her work. Was that too much to ask? Not knowing what to do next, she called up her best friend, Tanvi.

As soon as Tanvi picked up her call, Avni wanted to cry. She wanted to bawl like a child but containing herself, Avni whispered, 'Tanu,' and her lower lips trembled.

Tanvi could hear the pain in her best friend's voice. 'What's wrong?'

'I couldn't do it,' came Avni's defeated reply.

Tanvi sighed into her phone. 'Avni, listen to me and listen very carefully. No one is going to come swooping in. You have to do this on your own. If you want that individuality that you crave, then you have to work for it!'

Tanvi was so sure that this time around, her best friend would successfully break through. Tanvi couldn't exactly understand Avni's reasons to stay in her family like a prisoner when she could very well live on her own.

'Tanu…'

'No, Avni. I am not going to sympathise with you now. I admit that you had your reasons, and in the beginning, you weren't economically independent. But now, what reasons do you have? You say you aren't happy with your family. Until when are you going to groan and whine about the discriminatory behaviour of your family? You need to be a grown-up and face them!' And Tanvi hung up the phone. She knew that she was coming across as rude and inconsiderate. But when a gentle nudge doesn't help, then you have to give it a hard jerk. Tanvi's only hope was that this hard jerk worked.

Avni stared at her phone. Even her best friend wasn't willing to listen. She felt like she was drowning. She recalled Tanvi's words and felt like the biggest loser. She started cursing and name-calling herself.

'Stupid, that is what you are!' muttered Avni to herself.

'Who is stupid?' her mother, Sandhya Karamsheel asked from the doorway.

'Ma!' exclaimed Avni, 'No one,' she added hurriedly.

'Okay! I came to tell you that we have set up your profile on the matrimonial sites. We need a few good pictures,' her mother moved towards her cupboards taking out a saree and a *salwar kameez,* she added, 'You wear the saree first and come down. Ravi is downstairs waiting. He will click some pictures for the site,' and with that, Sandhya Karamsheel exited the room.

It was as if she hadn't said something life-changing. She delivered the information and completely wanted her daughter to follow suit. And being the dutiful daughter that Avni was trained into, she got up from the bed and started getting ready into the saree. It was as if Avni completely forgot that a minute ago she didn't want this.

After getting ready, Avni made her way down to the hall where Ravi was waiting. He clicked some ten photos of her. Some were of her sitting, some standing. Once done, her father told her to change into a *salwar kameez.* And same process was repeated.

Kadam Karamsheel selected five photos of his daughter in saree and *salwar kameez* for uploading on the matrimonial site. Once done, he rechecked the details he had filled in and then called his daughter. 'Come here, Avni. Take a look at your profile!' he said excitedly.

With slow steps, Avni made her way towards her father. She looked at the computer screen and mentally cringed. Her father had basically portrayed her as useless. Suddenly, she remembered Tanvi's words. *'Till when are you going to groan and whine?'*

In her room, Avni kept repeating Tanvi's words.

'Till when are you going to groan and whine?'

'Till when am I going to groan and whine?'

'I am going to be a grown-up and solve my problems!'

2

How Much Do You Earn?

What Avni needed was a plan of action. A plan of action to solve all her problems. And the first thing to do in her plan of action was to jot down all her problems. Yes, she would write about all her problems and issues and solve them all one by one.

'Avni, come on get ready,' her mother came barging into her room. She moved towards her cupboard, picked out a *salwar kameez*, placed it on the bed, clapped her hands, and said, 'Hurry up. We have to go to the temple,' and left the room.

Avni plopped down on her bed. She could feel her shoulders drooping, confidence shattering, but then, she shook her head and murmured, 'I need to be a grown-up!'

If her mother wanted to go to the temple, then so be it. If not her father, then she could start by telling the truth to her mother first.

Aren't they supposed to be more affectionate? Isn't the bond between a mother and a child considered sacred? And being a woman, she will surely listen to me. She would understand my wishes. Won't she? But I won't know until I try.

With determined thoughts, in the temple, Avni in a very timid voice mumbled, 'Ma, I need to talk to you about something,'

'Later.'

'It's important!'

'I said later,' hissed Sandhya Karamsheel.

Kusum Kashyap was shocked by Sandhya Karamsheel's attitude. Admittedly, Avni chose the wrong time to discuss something important, but her mother should have at least acted considerate. Instead, she was fuming, as if her child has committed some heinous crime. She saw Avni leave her mother's side. Kusum knew that this was her chance and she immediately followed Avni. There she was, standing near the drinking water area. Even from this far, Kusum could see that there were tears in her eyes. But Avni didn't let them fall.

Avni stood by the drinking water area, trying to compose herself. Once she was sure that not a single drop of her tear would fall out from her eyes, only then did Avni turn and grab a glass from the overhead cabinet. Another hand grabbed the same glass, and Avni turned her head to find a beautiful lady.

'I am sorry,' the lady moved her hand from the glass.

'No, I am sorry.' Avni too moved her hand away.

Chuckling, the lady said, 'You are sweet, Avni.'

How does the lady know my name?

'Don't you remember me? We met at your cousin's wedding ceremony,' the lady said.

Avni tried to recall but she couldn't remember meeting the lady. But the lady was looking at her so expectantly that she said, 'Of course, Aunty. How are you?'

Kusum flashed Avni a smile. She knew that the girl didn't remember her. How could she? They had never been properly introduced. 'I am Kusum Kashyap. Your father is friends with my husband.'

Taking another glass from the cabinet, Kusum went on to pour water from the tap. She very nonchalantly asked Avni, 'How are your studies going on?'

Avni gave her the deer caught in a headlight expression. Very awkwardly, she replied, 'Umm… I have completed my studies,' and forced a smile.

'Oh! I didn't know that. So, you must be doing a job?'

Avni didn't want to lie. Yet she had to. But before she could say something, 'Avni, there you are!' called out her mother.

'Ma, this is Kusum Aunty. Her husband and Dad are friends,' introduced Avni.

Sandhya hadn't seen Kusum there until Avni introduced them. She immediately masked a smile on her face and turned towards Kusum. 'Hi, I didn't see you there. I am Sandhya Karamsheel, Avni's mother. How have you been?'

Kusum merely nodded at her question and replied, 'I have been good.'

For the first time in her life, Avni was thankful to her mother for barging in. She didn't want to lie, not this time. There was something about Kusum Kashyap that attracted Avni. She didn't want to disappoint Kusum Aunty by lying to her.

While lost in her thoughts, Avni heard her mother say, 'Oh! Even we are looking for a groom for our Avni!'

'Are you both coming for the community prayer on Sunday?' asked a hopeful Kusum, changing the topic. For that was the only day when her son was probably free and could possibly accompany her. Kusum wanted Rithik to meet Avni because he liked the girl. This meeting would decide if her son was romantically interested in Avni or if it was just a mere curiosity.

Sandhya nodded her head. She had heard all about the Kashyaps from her husband. Kadam had told her that marrying Avni off to Kashyaps would be beneficial. But earlier in the week at the wedding ceremony, they had basically ignored Kadam. So, Kadam had struck them off the potential groom's list. But judging by Kusum Kashyap's body language, today Sandhya was sure that at least she was interested in getting Avni as her daughter-in-law. That meant Sandhya had to be there on Sunday. If she befriended Kusum, then maybe she could persuade her into an alliance among their kids.

'Of course, we will be here!' she beamed at Kusum.

*****

Rithik was about to begin his lunch when his phone pinged with an Instagram message alert. He tapped open the message and started reading it.

Dear Rithik,

Can I truly ask my intended groom about his salary? Won't he take offence? Isn't it said that a girl's age and a man's salary should never be discussed? I like this man, but let's be real, money is important. Like or love alone cannot feed you. We all need money.

Thanks in advance!
@missguided

Rithik chuckled at the question. It was an interesting way to put out such a simple question. Often, he had seen brides shy away from asking their groom about their salary. At least this one was curious. He furiously started typing on his phone.

Dear Miss Guided,

I must say, a cool username you got there. As your username, you are a little misguided. I believe the question you want to ask the man intended to be your groom is how much he earns. He might or might not take offence to your question but it's better to ask then and there than to pile up the questions in your mind. I cannot say why they said that a man's salary should not be discussed. But you are right that money is important; love alone cannot feed you. So, it's important that you know beforehand how much your groom earns. On the brighter side, if he doesn't take offence to your question then that could possibly mean that even he likes you.

I hope that you get to know how much your groom earns.

Wishing you a successful married life!

Dr Rithik D. Kashyap

@yourmarriageguide

'Rithik!' called out his mother as soon as he entered the house after a long tiring day at his office.

Rithik made his way towards the sofa in the hall where his mother was seated. He plopped down on the sofa and put his head on his mother's lap. There was something magical about that place. As if all his exhaustion, worries, and pain vanished right there when he lay his head on his mother's lap.

'Are you free this Sunday morning?' asked his mother gently massaging his head.

'Hmm… hmm.'

'Will you accompany me to the community prayer in the temple?'

'Hmm… hmm.'

'Rithik?' called out Kusum, unsure if her son was awake or asleep.

'Ma?'

'Are you sleeping?'

'No, Ma. I heard you loud and clear. You want me to accompany you to the community prayer on Sunday in the temple.'

'Okay! Okay!' Kusum was amazed that Rithik had readily agreed to accompany her to the temple.

Normally, Rithik avoided visiting the temple due to the fear of relatives. In fact, Rithik would create a huge fuss before going anywhere with her, let alone a temple. So, this was definitely a good sign. Maybe even the Gods were conspiring. If only they gave her a sign that Avni was the right one for her son. Her heart and mind said that Avni Karamsheel was it, but she couldn't ignore her husband's assessment of the Karamsheel family. Yet, so far, even she had liked Avni.

That night, Rithik couldn't sleep. After tossing and turning a lot in his bed, Rithik finally gave up. He grabbed his phone and popped open his Instagram. After scrolling through a few pages, he came across a food blogger page, Prashasti. Remembering the self-promise, he made earlier about eating healthy, Rithik scrolled through the page posts. Each food presented there looked so yummy. When he started reading the recipes in the caption section, he was surprised. All that delicious-looking food had the right amount of nutrition. He was impressed by the page. He made a quick note to show it all to Seema Di. The prospect of such delicious food made Rithik's stomach grumble. Getting up from the bed, he made his way towards the kitchen. He grabbed the cookie jar and poured himself a glass of milk and munched away. Once finished, he went back to bed and within minutes, he was fast asleep.

3

Are You Willing to Make It Work?

Rithik pulled open the door of the restaurant. He had come to the restaurant to meet Indra, his childhood buddy.

'Rithik, my man. How have you been?' Indra asked, hugging him.

'Good. What about you? How is Marie?' Rithik asked taking a seat.

Marie was Indra's wife. They had been together for eight years now. They dated for four years before Indra popped the big question. Marie was a gentle soul. Rithik has always enjoyed her company.

When he didn't get an answer from Indra, Rithik repeated his question, 'How is Marie?'

Breathing out, his friend finally said, 'Things have been a little strained between me and Marie.'

As a friend, it was unbelievable to Rithik that all wasn't well in Indra and Marie's marriage. But as a marriage therapist, he knew that every relationship had problems.

'What happened?' Rithik asked gently.

Indra started rubbing his jaw. Rithik had long ago read that tell of Indra's. Indra rubbing his jaw meant he wasn't sure if he should share his problems.

'Indra, I am your friend,' encouraged Rithik.

Indra bobbed his head. He knew that he could share his problems with Rithik, but still, there was uneasiness. Running a hand through his hair, he said, 'We have been trying for a kid for the past few months. Marie takes a test almost every month, and when it comes as a negative one, she… well, let's just say that Marie is more invested in this. It has started affecting our relationship. And… in between all this, Marie has lost herself. She… I love her. I don't know how I can help her. I want to give her that child she so badly craves. I feel so helpless!'

Indra sagged back in his seat. Rithik was his last hope. He hoped that his friend could mend the differences in his relationship with Marie. 'I am asking you as a client to help us out. I want my wife back. I want Marie back!'

'Okay. I… you…' Rithik wasn't sure if he should call his friend at the office. Marie and Indra were his friends. How can he be clinical about this? Controlling his emotions, Rithik finally said, 'Come to the office on Tuesday and bring Marie along. We will take it from there,' he patted Indra's hand.

Indra visibly relaxed. Lighting up the mood, Rithik said, 'Now, are we going to eat or what? I am hungry!'

Chuckling, Indra said, 'You place the order. You know what I like. I will just make a quick trip to the restroom.'

Rithik saw Indra leave the table. He thought about poor Marie. How distraught she must have been. He will have to do everything in his power to mend his friends' marriage.

Calling the waiter, Rithik placed the order, mini sandwiches for Indra and pasta for himself.

He sat back in his seat and glanced around.

Rithik's gaze fell onto a man at the next table. The man had an appalled look. He heard the man say, 'What kind of question is that?'

'A very valid one,' the girl's voice came out as soft yet firm. The girl had her back towards Rithik.

The man by now had turned into a funny shade of red. 'That is not something you ask your prospective spouse.' With that, the man left the table.

Rithik tsked. Call him old school, but he would have liked him to be at least chivalrous. The man could have at least paid the bill.

But the girl was least bothered by the man leaving. She made her way to the reception desk, probably asking for the bill. All the while, Rithik could see nothing more than her back.

As a marriage therapist, Rithik was now curious to know the question the girl had asked. He was just about to make his way towards the girl when Indra came back. He looked at his friend and then at the girl. His decision made him relax back in his seat. Rithik saw the girl leave the restaurant, and he prayed that she would at least turn. He wanted to catch a glimpse of her. But the only thing he saw was a birthmark or at least he believed it to be one. There was a wide dark patch under her wrist. It almost formed the shape of a heart. Rithik saw that when the girl had tucked a lock of hair behind her ear.

'Where are you lost?' Indra asked, waving a hand in front of Rithik.

'Mhm.'

Thankfully, the waiter arrived with their food.

'You know, it's amazing that you are willing to work out the problems in your marriage,' Rithik said, changing the topic. He had always liked people who were willing to make it work. It was another important factor in married life.

*****

Avni was pacing around in her room. So far, she had failed in her attempt to talk to her parents. So, she decided that she had to try a new approach.

'Avni!'

'Raashi Di, what are you doing here?' Avni had never really liked her cousin. Ever since Avni had turned eighteen, her cousin Raashi had been trying to marry her off to Rajesh, Raashi Di's far-removed brother-in-law. Also, Rajesh was almost forty while Avni was just twenty-five.

'What, no hug for your favourite cousin?'

Avni almost choked in Raashi's embrace. After releasing Avni, Raashi said, 'Come on, get ready. I am here to take you on a girl's day out. I have even taken your parents' permission!'

Avni sensed trouble, but keeping quiet, she did as she was asked. She always did what was asked of her.

Even after roaming around various shops, Raashi didn't buy a single thing. Avni's sense heightened. She was just waiting for the storm to come. She knew a storm was coming soon. She could very well read the signs of a storm coming. Raashi liked to shop, a lot. She remembered the time when Raashi had created a huge fuss because she wasn't able to find a perfect dress for an engagement party.

'Are you hungry? Let's eat!' said Raashi, pointing towards a nearby restaurant. Avni merely nodded and followed her inside the restaurant.

They were almost finished with their meal when Avni saw Rajesh walk in. And this was the storm that she had been waiting for.

'Avni!' Rajesh said, coming closer.

Raashi's phone rang at that exact moment. When Raashi excused herself to take the call, Avni knew that Rajesh meeting her at the restaurant was a planned one because Raashi never took a call in private.

Rajesh immediately plopped himself on the vacant seat and started off with his chats that Avni was least interested in. He told her about his business, his foreign trips, and the girls he rejected recently. 'Just for you, Avni,' he said, but Avni was sure that he was lying.

A 40-year-old man would never reject a girl's proposal if he ever received one!

Avni thought to herself as Rajesh finally blurted what he had come here for. 'Avni, don't you want me as your husband? I am rich. I can provide well for you. Ask me anything and get to know me. I am sure once you know me, you will be more than happy to marry me. I want you to marry me. Once you agree, I will even convince your parents!'

Wow, Rajesh was thinking way ahead. Suddenly, Avni had a question in her mind. She was sure that the question would take Rajesh running off in the other direction. Okay! The question would likely burn her also, but who cared? Moreover, working in the kitchen had made her skin so thick that she was sure that she wouldn't feel the pain. Jutting her chin up, she asked him the question.

As expected, Rajesh was appalled, 'What kind of a question is that?'

'A very valid one,' Avni's reply came out as soft yet firm.

'That is not something you ask your prospective spouse!' And with that, Rajesh left the table.

Avni glanced around, searching for Raashi. On not finding her in the restaurant, she made her way to the reception desk. When she asked for the bill, she was told that it was already paid. So Avni made her way out. She fished the phone out of her purse and called Raashi.

'Avni?' A bewildered Raashi called out from behind. 'Where is Rajesh?'

Shrugging, Avni just replied, 'He left,' and smiled.

Raashi was so sure that this time her plan would work. Ever since her marriage, she had been planning to marry Rajesh off to Avni. Rajesh was a thirty-eight-year-old bachelor. There was a running joke among her in-laws that marrying Rajesh off would be the noblest task anyone would have ever done. Raashi had taken it upon herself to complete the task. Marrying Rajesh off to Avni would give Raashi some standing among her in-laws. Of course, Rajesh had made that work easy by lusting after Avni. But then why would he leave so suddenly? Everything happened according to the plan. What could have possibly gone wrong to make Rajesh leave? Raashi peeked a glance towards Avni. She didn't look least bothered by this. Maybe Rajesh had some emergency to attend to. Why else would he leave so hurriedly? Yes, it had to be that.

'Okay! Let's go!' said Raashi, pulling Avni's hand.

For the next few hours, Avni lived in total fear. She waited for Rajesh to call Raashi and tell her about the question she had asked him earlier. But a day had passed, and Rajesh didn't call.

4

Will Adoption Be an Option?

When Rajesh didn't call her parents to complain about her question, two things were made clear to Avni. One was Rajesh's answer. Two, she still had it in her; the bold Avni was still there.

'Lord! Why aren't you ready?' her mother made a beeline for the cupboard.

This time Avni didn't even bother asking. She simply followed. As a result, she was standing in front of the temple forty-five minutes later. The blaring speakers made some announcements about the community prayer. It was then that things clicked in Avni's mind. Her mother had brought her for the Sunday community prayer. Which she rarely attended. They were just about to enter the temple when someone called out from behind, 'Sandhya, Avni!'

Avni saw her mother smile wickedly. 'Kusum. I didn't see you there. Did you come alone? Mr Kashyap didn't come along?'

Kusum Kashyap peeked a glance towards Avni, who was rolling her eyes at her mom's questions. She was trying to be subtle about it but was failing. 'No, no. I came with my son,

Rithik. He is parking the car.' Turning her head towards Avni, Kusum said, 'You met him at the wedding ceremony, remember?'

'Yes, and she was quite impressed,' Sandhya answered for her daughter.

Ushering them inside the temple, Kusum said, 'Come on. Let's go inside. I am also helping in the kitchen today. I need to check out things. Aren't you helping in the kitchen, Sandhya?'

Sandhya looked appalled by the thought of helping out in a community kitchen. But looking at Kusum's bright face, she knew she would have to help in the kitchen.

Avni coughed at Kusum's question. Her mother was a snob. She didn't like helping, let alone in a community kitchen. Trying to save her mother's face, Avni immediately said, 'I have urged Mom to let me take her place today.'

'What a sweet child you are!' said Kusum, gently patting Avni's cheek. To say that Avni was shocked by that gesture would be an understatement. She felt emotions pouring through her veins at that small gesture of Kusum Kashyap. For never had her mother or father patted her or told her that she was sweet. Avni's eyes welled up with tears.

Kusum couldn't understand the tears in Avni's eyes. She looked down at their feet, hoping that she hadn't stepped on her toe or something. Thankfully, she hadn't. When she looked up again at Avni's bright face, her tears were gone. But still, it bothered Kusum.

After the prayers, Kusum finally had Avni alone in the kitchen. She had so many questions to ask her. But Avni looked so peaceful and happy cooking that Kusum didn't have the heart to interrupt her. Avni was a great cook, thought Kusum. The aroma around was so rich and alluring.

It took two hours, but finally, the lunch was prepared. Kusum asked Avni to join her in gathering people around for lunch. Kusum's eyes were searching for her son. On spotting him, she waved him to come near.

Avni saw a very handsome man walking towards her. He looked like the young prince who was frequently pictured in fashion magazines.

'There you are,' the man said, coming near his mother.

Was he talking to her? Avni had almost asked him that question when Kusum Aunty beside her said, 'Rithik. You act as if I was lost!'

'I was, Mom. You have to save me from those aunties!'

Shit! He was Kusum Auntie's son?

Avni was supposed to know him.

But then, Kusum very cheerfully introduced Avni to her son. 'Rithik, meet Avni!'

Avni just wanted the ground to swallow her whole. The man, Rithik, turned to face her.

'Hi!' Avni said softly.

Kusum was very pleased to see her son's reaction when she introduced Avni. Rithik was staring at Avni as he would stare at his favourite dessert. So, she was right that her son was romantically interested in her. Now, her next task would be to tell the truth to her husband.

If in the moonlight she looked illuminating, then in the sunlight she looked radiant. Avni was nothing short of exquisite. Rithik couldn't take his eyes off her. He wondered if she remembered him. It wasn't like she had seen him back when they had first met on that terrace. His mom cleared her throat, forcing him to take his eyes off Avni.

Coming out of his dreams, Rithik gave a hand to Avni. 'Dr Rithik Dhananjay Kashyap.' He peered deep into her eyes.

When their hands touched, Rithik felt a zing pass through him. In that instant, Rithik saw his future with Avni. Rithik wasn't sure what was happening to him. But of one thing he was sure. Avni was not a mere curiosity.

Out of nowhere, Sandhya Karamsheel joined the group, souring Kusum's mood. Kusum cringed when Sandhya hooked her arm into her son's. Rithik too was taken by surprise.

'Rithik, how are you?' Even that simple question felt like Sandhya was spewing venom.

Rithik looked at his mother, hoping that she would rescue him from the overexcited aunty. But then, Avni very gently said, 'Mom.'

Rithik ran his free hand through his face. This overexcited aunty was Avni's mother.

Another aunty joined them. 'Aren't you all joining us for lunch?'

Kusum said, 'Yes, yes. Let's go!'

Thankfully now, Avni's Mom would have to unhook her arm from Rithik's. Because males and females were seated separately for lunch.

After lunch, despite Rithik's wishes, he had to leave for home. He tried so hard to find Avni, but she was nowhere to be found. Mother and son were almost at their car when Sandhya Karamsheel called out from behind, 'Kusum!' She briskly walked towards the car. 'I would have missed you. Phew. Anyway, I wanted to invite you to the game of archery. Please say you would come!' Turning towards Rithik, she continued, 'Even you must come, Rithik,' she smirked.

Chuckling, Kusum replied for both of them, 'We would, but tell us where and when!'

Sandhya quickly gave them the address. 'Next Sunday, you

must come!'

*****

On Tuesday, Rithik was waiting for his friends, Indra and Marie, to arrive. He was restless. This was new. He had never counselled relatives or friends.

'They are here,' his assistant said, peeking through the door.

'Send them in.' Rithik was tapping his fingers on the table.

The doors opened, and his friends came in. He got up and hugged Indra, giving a firm handshake to Marie. 'How have you been, Marie? Indra here has been keeping you all to himself.'

'I have been good, Rithik.' Marie immediately lowered her eyes.

'Let's take a seat,' Rithik ushered them onto the seats.

Rithik began the session by asking the couple about their problems. After half an hour of talking and listening, he got a clear picture of the situation. While Indra was willing to do anything to give Marie a child, Marie felt like she was failing Indra by not giving him one, even though both of them were medically not capable of having a child. Rithik didn't know that last piece of information. 'I didn't know that it was medically impossible for you both to have a child,' he said, looking at Indra.

Indra running a hand through his hair replied, 'I persuaded her to take a test over the weekend. The results came this morning.' He handed the report file to Rithik.

That could explain their defeated look. The wound was still fresh. 'Marie, you have to know that you are not at fault. You both are not medically fit to have a child, but that is okay, it happens,' Rithik said, taking her hand.

She softly started sobbing. A helpless Indra hugged her

sideways.

Rithik sighed and started slowly, 'Marie, if you really want a child, then…' Rithik hesitated but then looking at his friends' hopeful gazes, he said, 'I think you guys should look into adoption. If not the genes, then the values would be the same. You guys have so much love to give. I think you should keep adoption as an option,' he peered into her eyes.

Indra and Marie were now looking at each other as if silently asking if adoption was an option. Indra knew that Marie wanted a child. She wanted to be a mother and he would have done anything to make her happy. He even liked the idea of a kid in her arms. So, he nodded looking at her. And Marie's face lit up like the fourth of July. There it was, the thing that had been missing for the past few months, her bright smile.

The couple gave a warm look to Rithik. 'Thank you. Without you, I don't think we would have ever seen sense,' said Indra.

Chuckling, Rithik replied, 'You would have. It would have taken time. But you would have. I simply speeded up things. Now go and find me the prettiest niece and a dashing nephew. I am willing to have more than two but two is a must!'

Marie laughed so hard at Rithik's request that she had tears in her eyes. Indra was pleased to hear that laughter.

The couple got up and hugged Rithik. They finally made their way out of the office, hand in hand. Rithik had a bright smile on his face.

This was what he wanted with Avni.

Rithik shook his head. He had wondered when she would pop back into his mind. Ever since he had met her on Sunday, Avni had been present in his mind constantly. He couldn't seem to shake her off his mind.

5

Should I Get a Pre-Nuptial Contract Signed?

Sunday came faster than Rithik had hoped.

'Kusum, why did you have to agree to this?' whined his father for the hundredth time.

Rithik chuckled on hearing his parents crib at each other sweetly. While normally he would have joined his father, today he didn't. Today, he was excited to meet Avni again.

'I agreed because I liked Avni and her company,' Kusum said, getting out of the car.

Well, that was new! Nevertheless, Rithik was happy to know that his mother liked Avni and her company. Excitedly, he too got out of the car. He looked back to see his father dragging along. His father looked like a reluctant child on the first day of school.

He was almost at the door when his phone pinged with an Instagram message alert. He fished out the phone from his jeans pocket.

Dear Rithik,

I am a thirty-one-year-old businessman. I am rich and successful. I worked hard for that success. Recently, my family had been nagging me to get married. I liked the idea until someone mentioned that she would have half a say in my business empire. It's one thing to share your personal life, but must I share my business?

I would be thankful for your guidance.

@thestoicbusinessman

Instagram was the best thing Rithik had come across to connect with people. Often, we don't like to share our problems, especially personal problems. Instagram gave the option to remain anonymous. And the best part was a free consultation. Rithik would have helped out people for free if he didn't have to pay the bills.

Rithik scratched his jaw, thinking about his answer to @thestoicbusinessman's question.

Dear Stoic Businessman,

Marriage is a huge step, and just like the business you worked hard for, I hope that you work in a similar manner for your marriage. I hope that you have a long-lasting and successful married life.

Sharing your personal or professional life with your married partner should be your choice. I can understand your fears. I would suggest you ask your partner if she would be willing to sign a pre-nuptial contract.

For the right partner, it wouldn't matter. The right partner would willingly sign the contract. Even you might ignore that pre-nuptial contract with the right partner. But there is no harm in asking, right?

Best wishes!

Dr Rithik D. Kashyap
@yourmarriageguide

Once done, Rithik made his way inside the house. The house was a huge monstrosity. Things were totally out of place. But every item in the house screamed show off. That was it. This place was just a house, not a home.

'Rithik!' Kadam Karamsheel came out of nowhere and hugged Rithik. The Karamsheels were surely an over-excited bunch of people, thought Rithik. But then, a certain other Karamsheel popped into his mind. The shy and sweet one. Rithik's eyes roamed around searching for Avni.

Kusum was watching her son and Kadam Karamsheel from a distance. She nudged her husband.

An annoyed Krishna asked, 'What?'

With downcast eyes, Kusum began, 'Krishna, I have hidden something from you.' Looking back at her son, she continued, 'I think Rithik is romantically interested in Avni Karamsheel. That is why I have started hanging out with Sandhya Karamsheel. I didn't want to tell you earlier. I only wanted to tell when I was certain.' She looked at her husband hopefully.

Krishna's mouth hung open. In thirty years, his wife had never hidden anything from him. 'And now, you are certain, how?'

'You just have to look at our son to know that,' she replied, pointing towards their son.

Krishna looked towards the direction in which his wife had

pointed and surely, there he was, their son. He was talking to Kadam, but his eyes were searching for someone. Suddenly, his face lit up. Rithik was staring at something. Something had caught his attention; it was the reason for his lit face. Krishna followed Rithik's gaze and he saw a very pretty woman standing on the staircase. Beside him, Kusum whispered, 'That is Avni.'

Krishna nodded. His wife was right; their son was smitten. Krishna was in turmoil. As if sensing his dilemma, his wife said, 'Avni is a nice young woman. Nothing like her parents, at all!'

Avni was furiously walking down the stairs. She had been trying so hard to talk to her parents, but they had, like always, been ignoring her. They had the time to host this stupid game but not listen to their only daughter. She was fuming mad.

But then, something to her right caught Avni's attention. It was Rithik. He was here. He came.

'Avni, there you are. Come, meet Rithik,' her father called out.

She barely made a step in their direction when her mother called out from the kitchen, 'Avni, I need your help!'

Rithik was so mad right now. He had barely managed to say more than his name to Avni. He wanted to talk to her, know her. How else would he decide that she was the one?

'Never mind, you can meet her later. Come, let's start the game.' With that, Kadam Karamsheel led them to the backyard.

They were midway through the game when a guy said, 'I met this girl last night. She was all pretty and dolled up, but when she started talking about prenuptial contracts, I ran for my life. I mean, man, you don't want to sign those and lose all your money!'

All the other guys around Rithik chuckled. Even Kadam Karamsheel chuckled.

'I don't think it was wrong of her to ask about it. For all we know, she could be worried that you would take over her assets. After all, a woman has a right in her parents' properties now,' remarked Rithik.

Avni, who was listening to this discussion from the doorway, was pleasantly surprised. Never had she met a man who had considered a woman as someone equal.

'Yes, yes,' said Kadam Karamsheel, even though he didn't agree with Rithik. Kadam Karamsheel's only agenda was to marry Rithik and Avni. Ever since Sandhya had told him about Kusum Kashyap's possible interest in Avni, Kadam had been plotting as to how he would forge an alliance between the two families.

'He is a marriage therapist,' Avni heard Kusum behind her.

'Oh! He is the marriage guide that everyone has been talking about!' asked another voice.

'Sorry?' said Kusum.

'The one on Instagram. He is really good and has been gaining followers with each passing day!'

Avni zoned out after hearing that Rithik was on Instagram. That meant she could stalk him there. She was just about to start her stalking but stopped herself. She thought about doing it alone in her room at night. When she wouldn't be interrupted.

The rest of the day passed in a blur for Avni. She was too excited to pay attention to anything and too focused on her goal to stalk Rithik on Instagram.

By evening, all the guests had left the house. With each passing second, Avni grew more restless. She couldn't understand this feeling. Why was she so excited to stalk Rithik on social media?

Isn't stalking wrong? But I am not harming him. So, it couldn't be considered wrong. Could it?

That night, Avni rushed through her dinner. Her parents, as usual, didn't notice anything unusual. But right now, she was least bothered by anything. She felt like she had started craving Rithik like pizza or any fast food.

Finally, in her bed, Avni popped open her Instagram account. She searched for Rithik Dhananjay Kashyap. There was only one account with that name, and he was following her, Prashasti.

Why was he following me? What interested him?

Ignoring her questions, Avni opened Rithik's page. Rithik's profile picture was of him in a *kurta pyjama*. He looked so dashing. She scrolled through. There were pictures of him in various stages and places. There were screenshots of the messages seeking help and his reply to those messages. Avni read those posts. She was surprised by Rithik's insight.

She thought about the question she had asked Rajesh. Avni wondered what Rithik's insight on that question would be. While deciding whether she should ask Rithik the question or not, Avni slept, with Rithik's page still wide open on her phone.

*****

Rithik was in a sour mood after he returned home. He had gone to the Karamsheel's house with the hope to meet Avni, to get an opportunity to interact with her and get to know her better. He instead got over-excited aunties or orthodox uncles for company. If that wasn't enough, then there was that vile man who thought that it was a joke to sign prenuptial contracts.

Rithik opened his Instagram account on the phone and started scrolling. He was in need of something good. Suddenly, he remembered that food blogger's account. He opened her page and started saving the recipes he would like to try. Rithik liked to cook but time didn't permit him to. Once he was done saving the recipes, he felt somewhat relaxed. And like always, his relaxed mind wandered off to Avni. He wondered when she would leave his mind.

6

How Often Are You Willing to Do the Housework?

The next morning, Rithik was confused. He had a hundred missed calls, and about two hundred text messages, and his Instagram was flooded with questions.

'Rithik!' His mother was banging on his bedroom door.

Jumping immediately to his feet, he pulled open the door. 'Ma, is everything alright?'

'Why don't you tell us? There is a throng of people with cameras standing outside our house. Some I believe are paparazzi. They have been calling out your name!' explained his mother.

Rithik was now baffled. *What had happened?* He looked at his mother who had a similar expression. His father joined them. 'Man, what exactly did you do? Tell me you didn't do something illegal. These people came early in the morning and haven't left since!'

'I didn't do anything. I don't know what is happening!'

Running back towards the nightstand, Rithik grabbed his phone and opened his messages.

'Dr Kashyap, are you the face behind the page, Prashasti?'

'Rithik, how do you know Prashasti?'

'Dr Kashyap, would you be willing to give us an interview?'

'Rithik, thank you for such amazing food recipes!'

'A cook in the garb of the marriage therapist. Nice going, man!'

'Rithik, why the name Prashasti?'

The puzzle around him finally started to fit. It was all linked to the food blogger's page, Prashasti.

Rithik immediately messaged Prashasti on Instagram asking what was happening. But he didn't get a reply. He tossed his phone. 'I think it has something to do with a food blogger page that I follow,' explained Rithik to his parents.

'Food blogger page?' asked his curious Mom.

'Yes, Ma. You have been nagging me to eat healthy. So, I thought I would take some extra help. Besides her page looked so delicious that I couldn't ignore it!'

'Show me,' Kusum and Krishna said at the same time. Rithik grabbed back his phone and showed the page to his parents.

'These look so delicious,' remarked his father.

'And healthy too,' commented his mother.

'See, I told you, hard to ignore,' Rithik told his parents.

Nodding, his parents left him alone. He had to go to his office but with the chaos around him, Rithik wasn't sure if he could. So, he called his assistant and told him to make the necessary changes. Since he was home again today, he thought about cooking. After all, the whole fuss started because of food. Yes, he would cook something from Prashasti's page.

After freshening up, Rithik made his way down to the

kitchen. 'Seema Di, come on, out. I will cook today, and you will eat it.' He shoved the cook out of the kitchen.

*****

On the other side of the city, Avni got up to a similar scenario. The only difference was that all her missed calls and messages were from her best friend, Tanvi.

She immediately called her back. 'Tanvi?'

'What did you do, Avni?' Tanvi barged on her.

'Why did you do it?' she continued, 'What were you thinking? Did you tell your parents? Was that why you did it? Are your parents angry? Do you want me to come over?'

Her best friend was on fire! She had so many questions. But Avni didn't have the answer to a single question. A puzzled Avni asked Tanvi to take a deep breath. 'Now tell me what exactly I did.'

'You followed an account on Instagram.'

Avni wasn't sure that she heard it right. So, she asked her again, 'I did what?'

'You heard me the first time, Avni,' replied Tanvi.

No, no. This was not happening. How did that happen?

Avni was never supposed to follow another account. Now the paparazzi would come looking for her. Her secret would be out before she even got the chance to tell her parents. They would get furious. She had to do something. Control the damage. She was just about to open her Instagram account and unfollow the person when Tanvi spoke, 'Do you even know this Dr Rithik Dhananjay Kashyap?'

Avni gasped out loud, 'I might have followed him last night by mistake!'

'Mistake?'

'Hmm…' Anvi took a deep breath as she started, 'Listen carefully. I was stalking him, Tanvi. I must have slept with the page open and tapped on the follow button,' said Avni, running a hand through her hair.

'You got a crush on someone, and you didn't tell me?' squeaked Tanvi.

Is that what it is called? This unstoppable need to see him, know him, or talk to him.

'Uhh…' hesitated Avni, 'I wasn't sure if you were mad at me or not.'

'I am mad, and I will be till you don't tell your parents about Prashasti. But that does not mean that you can hide things from me,' chided Tanvi.

Avni nodded. On realising that Tanvi couldn't see her nodding over a voice call, she whispered, 'Okay.'

After a moment, Avni asked, 'Should I unfollow him?'

'No. That would raise suspicion. Let it be,' advised Tanvi.

Avni gently asked her best friend, 'Are you really mad at me?'

'Okay bye! I will talk later.' With that Tanvi kept the phone, giving Avni her answer. Tanvi was still mad. Avni would have to do something about that. But before that, she needed to clear out the mess she created last night.

Avni's phone pinged with an Instagram message alert. It was Rithik. He was confused and wanted to know what was happening. The paparazzi were bugging him. She debated whether she should respond to him or not. But he had the right to know why he was bothered by the paparazzi. So, Avni started typing a reply.

Dear Rithik,

I am sorry to know that the paparazzi have been bothering you and your family. I am sorry for the mess I sent your way. I never really meant to follow you or anyone. It happened last night by mistake. I was tired and already in bed when I was scrolling through Instagram and came across your page. It didn't feel right to unfollow you this morning. I hope my recipes would compensate.

@prashasti

She had barely sent the message out when her phone pinged with his reply.

Dear Prashasti,

Thank you for the explanation. One does not wish to get up to a throng of paparazzi waiting outside the house. I forgive you. I don't have an issue if you wish to unfollow me even now. Yes, your recipes are certainly helping. I just hope they turn out as delicious as they look on your page.

Dr Rithik D. Kashyap
@yourmarriageguide

Rithik made Avni curious with that last statement of his. Now, even she wanted to see if her recipe turned out as something delicious. She was just hoping that Kusum Aunty liked her recipe.

Dear Rithik,

Ask your mother to click a picture and give feedback once she is done preparing the meal.

@prashasti

Avni immediately got Rithik's reply.

Dear Prashasti,

Why would you think that it's my mother doing the cooking? I am preparing the meal. And yes, I will send you the picture along with feedback.

Dr Rithik D. Kashyap
@yourmarriageguide

Avni was rendered speechless. Do such men really exist? Yes, Tanvi had once told her that they did but she never believed her. How could she? No men in her family did the housework, ever. They always ask the women in the family to do it. They didn't even lift their hand for a glass of water. They would call out to a woman to give them a glass of water. If only the men in her family were like Rithik and his family.

With each day, she learned something new about him and it warmed Avni up. She wondered if he was a great cook. Oh! How she wished to know more about him. They had yet to share more than a "hi" and their names. Well, they might have just known their names until now, but of one thing, Avni was clear that

Rithik was willing to do housework.

What was it that Tanvi had said? A crush. But a crush wasn't the right word to describe what Avni felt for Rithik. She felt something deeper for him. There was a pull, cosmic energy, call it whatever you want to, but it was more. She was shocked by this intense feeling for him. Yes, this feeling was beyond a crush. She wondered if Rithik felt the same.

It was some two hours later, and Avni was in her room working on her recipe book when her phone pinged with an Instagram message alert. Rithik had messaged her the photos. He even sent her a wiped-out plate photo. He had captioned that one "It was plate-licking!"

Avni had a huge grin on her face. This was what she had always aimed for when she created those recipes. A healthy and tasty meal. She glanced at the book on the desk. The one she had been creating. She hadn't even told Tanvi about this recipe book. She had been working on it for quite some time now. Earlier, she wanted to dedicate it to her parents, hoping that they would listen to her and be proud of her. But judging by how her parents had been ignoring her, she wasn't sure about it now. Now she just wanted to tell them the truth and be done.

7

What If Your Family Wronged Me?

'I have heard that the Karamsheels have finally found the man for Avni,' Kusum said, sitting down for dinner.

Rithik froze in his seat. He knew that they were looking for a groom, but he didn't know that they were actively looking. His gut twisted at the thought of Avni marrying someone else.

Kusum peeked a glance towards her son. She knew that Rithik was interested in Avni, but he had been too slow to act upon it. Kusum had lost all her patience. Earlier this week, when she heard through grapevine that the Karamsheels were aiming to land an NRI as their son-in-law, Kusum knew that she had to act fast.

'You know, I think even you should marry, Rithik,' remarked Kusum offhandedly.

'Okay!' replied Rithik.

'Did you just agree?' His mother looked at him perplexed.

Rithik just shrugged.

'Are you in love with someone? Do you have a girl in mind?' asked his father.

Rithik thought that this was his chance. He had to confess. He must tell his parents about Avni.

Taking a deep breath, Rithik said, 'I do like someone. But I am not sure if she likes me or will even be willing to marry me.'

Kusum almost jumped up from her seat. She had been waiting for this exact moment. But keeping her emotions in check, she said, 'Don't you advise your clients to ask questions? There is no harm in asking. If you don't ask, then how will you know? You might miss your chance!'

Rithik couldn't breathe. The thought of not having Avni in his life was too painful for him to bear. 'I like Avni Karamsheel!' he snapped.

His mother was now grinning ear to ear. 'I know,' Kusum said, getting up and hugging her son.

'You know?' Rithik looked at his mother suspiciously.

Sitting back in her chair, his mother said, 'I have had my suspicions that you liked her. So, I tried to get you two to meet!'

That explained the temple and the game of archery.

With a defeated look, Rithik said, 'Ma, I don't know a thing about her apart from her name. I want to spend some time with her before I can decide if I want to marry her.'

Shaking his head, his father said, 'But that's the beauty of love, son. You don't need to know the name. Sometimes it just takes one look to fall in love. Sometimes even a lifetime is not enough to fall in love!'

Am I in love?

'You don't worry about a thing. I will arrange some private time for both of you.' Kusum knew that Sandhya would only be happy to help. Even the orthodox Kadam Karamsheel would agree. Kusum would make sure.

*****

'Okay, I will see you soon.' With that, Sandhya Karamsheel kept the phone. 'Your plan worked. That was Kusum Kashyap. She wants to meet us. She even specifically asked you to be present. Krishna Kashyap would also be joining,' she informed her husband.

Kadam knew that this would work. A small lie was all it took for Krishna to come running at Kadam's feet. He smirked at that thought. Kadam never liked the way Krishna had treated him back in college. As if Kadam was some lowly creature. He knew Rithik was interested in Avni, and that was why the Kashyaps were now trying very hard to get in touch. Now Krishna would have to beg for this relationship before he would agree.

'Why are you so hell-bent on this boy?' Sandhya asked her husband. She had known long ago not to question her husband's decision. But something was not sitting right with her. Maybe her maternal instincts were finally kicking in.

Kadam stared at his wife. She dared to question him. Getting up, he grabbed Sandhya by the hair and forced her to look him in the eye. 'You have no right to question me. You do as I say. Do not question me. Am I clear?'

Sandhya watched the retreating back of her husband. Sometimes she wondered how her life would have been if she had married someone else. Like the guy who had liked her, even Sandhya had liked him. But Sandhya came from a poor family, and she had no choice but to marry Kadam, who was rich. At least her family was taken good care of. She shuddered at the thought of her mother-in-law. Even from the grave, she continued to haunt her. Even now, she could hear her taunts. Sandhya didn't even want to think of her father-in-law, who had once tried to sexually assault her. She had poked the man in the eye and escaped. When she told her husband, Kadam merely brushed it off. As if it wasn't anything of importance. That day was the turning point in her life. She distanced herself from everyone. She merely started existing. After being poked in the eye, her father-in-law also left her alone and in peace. Sandhya remembered the day Avni was born. For a moment, she had felt happy. She even thought about living and not merely existing. But then her mother-in-law had taunted Sandhya about not having a son. And just like that, Sandhya went back to existing.

'Ma, I need to talk to you,' said Avni from the doorway.

'Not now. We have guests coming over,' said her mother, getting up from the couch.

Avni wanted to argue. But for the first time in her life, she saw something different in her mother's eyes. Something more than a social bee. There was something almost motherly about her mother today. So, she nodded and left.

Considering that it was already six in the evening, Avni was sure that the guests were coming over for dinner.

Avni was almost ready when she heard a voice. She could have sworn that it was Rithik's voice. Rithik… every time Avni thought about him, she would get this weird feeling in her stomach. If there was something that interested her more than being in a kitchen, then it was Rithik. And that was a scary feeling for Avni, but even then, she felt a weird calmness within her whenever she was around Rithik.

Avni was almost on the last step of the stairs when she saw Rithik, and her steps faltered. She was sure that she was going to land on the hard floor, but instead, she was pulled into a hard chest.

'Are you alright?' Rithik asked her, tucking a lock of Avni's hair behind the ear.

When Avni nodded, Rithik straightened her. Rithik itched to pull Avni closer. She looked so pretty in the green salwar kameez. She had even applied kohl on her eyes, just like the day when he had first met her at the wedding ceremony.

Once they were seated at the dinner table, only then did Krishna begin. 'I will cut to the chase, Kadam. We like Avni. We want her and Rithik to spend some time together and get to know each other. If God willing, then maybe even marry each other,' he smiled.

Rithik almost wanted to laugh at his father for the blunt manner in which he spoke. He was worried that Kadam Karamsheel might take his father's blunt attitude as rude behaviour. He peeked a glance towards Avni, wondering what she was thinking. She had her best poker face on. He couldn't even guess what Avni was thinking.

Avni almost had a no on the tip of her tongue for Mr Kashyap's request. But she knew that she wasn't supposed to utter a word in front of the guest unless she was asked a direct question. So, she zoned out of the conversation going around her.

After a few minutes, she finally focused back on the conversation. She heard her father say, 'I will only agree to your request if you agree to do an engagement ceremony.' And just like that, her fate was sealed.

'You didn't even ask your daughter about her wish, Uncle,' Rithik pointed out. Hearing that warmed Avni's heart. He had at least considered, unlike her father who didn't even bother.

Chuckling, her father replied, 'I know my daughter, son. Trust me when I say that your feelings are reciprocated.'

Avni jerked her head up only to find Rithik's eyes on her. He was staring at her intently. As if asking her if that was true. She looked around and found that everyone had a similar expression.

Not knowing what to do next, she mumbled, 'Excuse me,' and dashed towards her bedroom.

'Didn't I tell you? My Avni is a shy little girl,' said Kadam.

Rithik wasn't sure what to make out of that statement. Yes, he had seen Avni as a meek, shy, little girl, but her eyes, they told him a different story. Whenever he looked into her eyes, he saw a fierce woman. Someone capable of leaving her mark on the world. Someone full of love and life.

8

Condoms Or Contraceptive Pills?

It had been two months now. Two months since that article about Prashasti came out, Avni had still not managed to tell her parents about it. She wondered if it was similar for other kids. She thought about whether other kids also had to beg for some alone time with their parents. The only good thing that came out in these two months was Rithik. He was so different from her parents and family. Although she wasn't sure if she wanted to marry Rithik, she hadn't said a word. How could she? No one in her family bothered asking her. Surprisingly, time and again, Rithik and his parents had asked her if Avni wanted to marry him. She had never been able to answer that question truthfully to the Kashyaps with her parents chaperoning her meeting with them. Yes, Avni's parents always chaperoned her meeting with either Rithik or his parents. Avni hadn't even talked to her best friend about any of this. She hadn't talked to Tanvi for two months apart from that one time when Tanvi had called to enquire about the single follow, Rithik, on her Instagram page Prashasti.

Adjusting her dress, Avni thought that she was nothing less than a coward for blindly following her parents. She was exactly like her parents described her, meek. A meek little girl. She was making a life-changing decision, and based on what? Her parents told her to do so.

The cousins who had helped Avni get ready exclaimed and told her that she made the prettiest bride. Once done, those cousins guided her down the stairs.

'There she is,' exclaimed her mother. The group of women surrounding her "ahh"ed and "ooh"ed on seeing Avni.

She heard someone say, 'You are lucky to land Rithik Dhananjay Kashyap as your son-in-law, Sandhya.'

Another aunty joined, 'You will be the talk of the society after this union!'

'When are the Kashyaps coming in for the engagement ceremony?' enquired someone.

That question finally started to sink in Avni. She was getting engaged today. She was getting engaged to be married off. She was making a lifelong commitment today. She hadn't even called her best friend to this life event, and her parents hadn't even bothered to inform Tanvi. She wished for so many things right now. But then, suddenly, the dhol started playing, and in came Rithik.

Avni couldn't tear her gaze off Rithik. He looked like he had come out straight from the Regency period. The sherwani might have given Rithik some added appeal but he could easily pass off as a Maharaja any day.

Rithik just wanted a simple ceremony, not this whole drama. But the Karamsheels were adamant, and his father agreed. The beat of the dhol around him was giving Rithik a headache. But then his gaze fell onto Avni, and his headache vanished, poof!

Rithik was joined by a few giggling aunties. They started the welcoming ceremony before the engagement. In their fits of giggles, some aunty said, 'Now you are about to marry our Avni. Don't you dare give her some pills to prevent having children! We want those children!'

Was this aunty for real? Now, Rithik knew that he should have kept quiet and let that comment slide. For that was how these aunties rolled, poking their noses in others' business.

But then he looked up at Avni and she had a fearful expression on her face. 'First of all, Aunty, this is a private matter which I don't wish to discuss with my parents, let alone you. The only person with whom I would be discussing children would be my wife, Avni. Second, it has to be entirely Avni's decision if she wants a child. She will be the one bearing the pain. She has the complete right to decide if and when she wants a child. The third and final thing, I would never give her any pills which have known side effects, especially when there is an alternative. Her well-being is my top priority. Even if I have to compromise, I will, for her well-being. I will be marrying her, not buying her. She is an individual, and I don't want her to lose that individuality by forcing any kind of decision on her. She is free to do as she wishes. My only wish is to share her life. Not impact her individuality in any way. I hope I was clear enough,' he smiled.

Rithik hadn't realised that everyone present was listening to him. There was complete silence in the house. He had only meant for Avni to listen. He wanted to reassure her, get that fearful look off her face.

Would he really be willing to compromise? Would her individuality not matter to Rithik? What would he say if she told him about Prashasti? Avni had so many questions she wanted to ask Rithik. But neither was she given time nor the privacy to ask those questions.

'Let's begin the ceremony,' Kadam Karamsheel said, breaking the silence. Everyone gathered around the small dais set up for the engagement ceremony to take place.

Her mother guided Avni to the dais. Even Kusum Aunty came around to help her. Avni was wearing a heavy lehenga without assistance she was likely to fall flat on her face.

When she came face to face with Rithik, Avni heard Tanvi's voice, 'No one is going to come swooping in!' and she almost started looking for her best friend in the crowd when she realised that she hadn't even invited her best friend.

Avni was given a ring. She had to place the ring on Rithik's ring finger. She raised the ring in one hand and asked for Rithik's hand from the other. She was almost there. She could do it. Avni just had to place the ring. But she couldn't. Dropping her shoulders in defeat, Avni looked up into Rithik's eyes. 'I cannot marry you.' She heard people around her gasp. But Rithik was gleaming. There was happiness in his eyes.

'Avni, what are you saying?' demanded her father.

'The truth, Dad. The truth!' Avni turned back to Rithik.

'Rithik, I am not what my parents have told you. I am a successful woman in my own right. The food blogger page that you follow is actually mine. I am Avni Prashasti Karamsheel. Of course, my best friend, Tanvi, also manages the page, but the recipes are mine. It didn't feel right not to tell you this!'

'What did you say?' it was her father. But she was waiting for Rithik's reaction.

Rithik knew it! He knew that there was something more behind that meek exterior. He mentally fist pumped. He was just about to tell her that "it didn't matter" when he saw a hand come across Avni. Her father was about to hurt her. But on time, Rithik grabbed that hand and shoved it away. Avni immediately took a step back and she would have fallen, had he not pulled her into him.

'You okay?' he asked Avni gently.

When she nodded, he straightened her and said, 'It doesn't matter to me, Avni. Actually, it does; your recipes are amazing. I have tried ten of them by now, and they turned out to be super tasty!'

Avni was so happy that Rithik was taking her news so calmly, unlike her father, who had tried to hit her. It was then that Avni finally decided that it was time. She had to cut ties with her parents and family. They were nothing short of toxins. She had to break free.

Crouching down, she looked at the man who was responsible for her birth. This man was supposed to love her unconditionally. But Avni was sure that the element called love was missing from his soul. He was rude, arrogant, and a show-off. He never loved her. Yet, she had continuously sought his approval. But for what? To be degraded?

'You heard me the first time, Dad. I am not marrying a man of your choice. I am not the little girl you have asked me to play repeatedly! If you can't see me as a grown-up woman, then that's your problem.'

Kadam raised his hand to slap Avni. But she grabbed the hand before it could hit her cheek. 'Today, you lose the right to be my father. You are nothing to me from here on. You and your family are nothing to me!'

'We are nothing? The fifteen-minute fame has got into your head. Try surviving without us in the world,' sneered Kadam.

'I bet it would be better than anything you have to offer!' countered Avni.

Avni might have faced her biggest fear. But rather than feeling triumphant, she had mixed emotions. She wanted her father to see sense. But she knew it was too late now. That window would now forever remain closed. However, a new door has just opened for her. And she had to walk towards it. Excitedly, Avni made her way towards the door.

She was just at the door when her father said from behind, 'Leave the clothes and pieces of jewellery behind.'

Giving a sinister laugh, Avni turned around. 'Just so you know, this,' she gestured at the clothes and pieces of jewellery she was wearing, 'has been bought from my money. Ever since I have been earning, I stopped using the credit card you gave me!'

Rithik was so pleased by Avni. She looked like she was ready to take the world. He jogged behind her. 'Avni, wait!'

Behind him, Rithik's parents also followed.

Avni wasn't sure where she was going but she knew that she wasn't coming back to this house. She almost made it to the main gate when she heard, 'Avni, wait!'

Turning around, Avni found Rithik and his parents. Even now, her parents hadn't come. 'I am sorry, Rithik. I… I just need… I am not sure what I want right now.'

Coming near, Rithik wiped Avni's tears. 'You did nothing wrong, Avni. Take all the time you need. I am willing to wait!' he smiled at her.

Kusum went on to hug Avni. 'Do you have somewhere to go? You can stay with us if you want.'

Avni almost started weeping at her kind gesture. Here was a complete stranger willing to help her as her family, especially when her own father had kicked her out.

Avni was standing outside the Karamsheel house, still pondering over her next step, when she saw her mother coming towards her. Avni wondered what she had to say when she didn't utter a word in front of her husband. For as long as Avni could remember, Sandhya Karamsheel had always been like that. She had let her husband walk all over her. Was she here to add more insults?

But when a hesitant Sandhya opened her mouth, she surprised everyone. 'At least you were brave enough. Be happy. Live your life. I am proud of you!' she turned and went inside the house.

Was that really her mother? Did she finally say the words that Avni had wanted to hear for a long time? Her mother was proud of Avni. She wasn't sure what to make out of it.

'Come, we will go home,' said Rithik.

'Uhh…' She didn't want to impose on the Kashyaps. The only person she knew that she could impose on right now was Tanvi.

'I have a friend living nearby. I… would you mind dropping me there?' She asked, looking up at Rithik's handsome face.

9

Do You Wash Your Underwear?

Rithik didn't like the idea one bit. He didn't like leaving Avni behind with a friend, but he promised her that he would give her time and now he must. He very casually asked Avni, 'Who is this friend you are talking about?'

'Tanvi.' Avni looked out of the car, the trees passing by. She was sure that Tanvi would help her. What Avni worried about was Tanvi's reaction to her almost engagement party. 'Take a left,' she told Rithik.

Avni was fidgeting with her dress after pressing the doorbell of Tanvi's house. Why was she nervous? This was her best friend. Avni knew she was unnecessarily worrying but she couldn't calm herself.

'Avni?'

Avni was unsure of what she should do or say. She simply jumped on her best friend. 'I am sorry, Tanu,' she was on the verge of crying.

Tanvi looked behind Avni to find a very attractive man patiently waiting. She pulled her best friend, 'What's wrong?'

'I… I am sorry!' Avni hiccupped the words.

'Come on, in,' Tanvi felt the man follow. Who was he? With each passing second, Tanvi felt anxious.

'I told him,' Avni mumbled taking the glass of water from Tanvi. She waited for the words to sink in her best friend. When they did, Tanvi finally squeaked, 'You did?'

When Avni nodded, Tanvi hugged her. Oh! How long she had waited for this day. 'How, when, what did he say? Who is this man you brought along?' Tanvi whispered to her friend.

'Umm…Tanu, this is Rithik, my almost fiancé,' Avni said, looking at the man. A fuming Tanvi looked at the man, and then at Avni. 'You are getting married?'

Avni knew that she deserved Tanvi's anger, but she didn't wish Rithik to witness Tanvi's wrath.

'I… I should just go. Take care, Avni. Call me for anything,' Rithik said uncomfortably.

'Why didn't you tell me?' demanded Tanvi.

'I didn't know what I was doing, Tanu. But it was your words that stopped me from going ahead. It was you and the distance that you created between us that finally made me confess!'

Tanvi wanted to stay mad, but she couldn't. 'I am so sorry for not being there,' she muttered.

Taking her best friend's hand, Avni said, 'Even I am sorry!'

*****

Rithik had given Avni one week of space. Every day, he wanted to call her, but he knew that she needed some time to process it all. Also, he was secretly hoping that she would contact him. But today, he was losing his patience. He wanted to meet her.

He was outside the house he had last left Avni. He mentally cursed himself for never daring to ask for her phone number. If only he had braved her father. No, no. It was better that he hadn't.

He rang the doorbell.

'Rithik?' exclaimed Tanvi pulling open the door.

'Umm… I am… Avni… is she here?' God alone knew why he was stuttering.

'Yes, yes. Come on in.' Tanvi ushered Rithik inside the house. Pointing towards the sofa, she said, 'Take a seat. I will go call her. She was taking a bath. So, it might take some time.'

'Umm… Tanvi… tell her not to rush on my account. I will wait.' Rithik was tapping his fingers on each other.

Rithik was exactly as Avni had described him, patient and calm. Tanvi quickly made her way to Avni's bedroom. 'Avni, are you done?'

'Yeah,' replied Avni, pulling open the door.

'Rithik has come to meet you!'

'What?' Avni almost shrieked.

'He is waiting in the hall,' Tanvi beamed.

'I am not even dressed!' Avni said, panicking.

'Then you must!' suggested Tanvi and exited Avni's room.

Tanvi was smiling wide. Ever since she had known that there was no one in the world for her, that she was an orphan, Tanvi hadn't let anyone into her world. But Avni, she was special. She made her see dreams. Tanvi was only delighted to help Avni in her journey of life. Avni was the single person who stood by Tanvi's side, and who held her when she cried. It was only fitting that Tanvi helped Avni. She regretted that she had to be harsh to

Avni, but Tanvi had no other option.

'What are you doing standing there?' asked Avni, coming out of her room.

Tanvi hadn't even realised that she was standing against a wall and lost in her past. 'Nothing. Come let's meet that handsome hunk of yours!' she held Avni's arm and pulled her excitedly.

'He is not my handsome hunk,' Avni told Tanvi. But the blush on Avni's cheeks told a different story.

Rithik got up from the couch when he saw Avni. 'Hi.'

'Hi.'

'I will leave you two,' said Tanvi, rolling her eyes. She was happy for her best friend. She genuinely was, but she had no desire to be the third wheel in their relationship.

'I am sorry for coming here without informing you. But Ma was worried, and we didn't have your phone number,' Rithik said nervously.

'Oh, it's okay, Rithik. Come, have a seat.' Avni outstretched her hand towards the couch. It was then that Rithik's gaze fell onto her wrist. He looked up into her and back at that heart-shaped mark under her wrist. How had he missed it until now?

Taking a seat, Rithik finally blurted, 'What question did you ask that man in the restaurant?'

'I am sorry?' Avni's brows narrowed.

Shit! Rithik hadn't meant to blurt it out. 'I am sorry. It's just that…' He took her hand in his and started tracing the mark. 'How did you get this?'

'It's a birthmark,' Avni whispered hoarsely.

'Sometime back, I had seen you in a restaurant. You had a meeting with someone, probably a prospective groom.'

Avni understood where Rithik was going with this, but he

needed to stop tracing her birthmark if he wanted answers. She jerked her hand. 'I…' She took a deep breath, trying to calm the burning desire to touch her birthmark. She felt her face burning up. She took another breath. 'I wasn't meeting someone. Rajesh invited himself.'

Nodding, Rithik asked, 'What question did you ask him? He was ready to blow up any moment!' he grinned.

Blushing, Avni replied, 'I… I asked him if he washed his own underwear,' and smiled meekly.

The marriage therapist in him was rendered speechless. The man in him was impressed. The human in him was proud of Avni. Rithik smiled up at her. 'You are a brave woman, aren't you?'

Avni was stunned that Rithik didn't have a counter-question like 'Why that question? What is the significance of that question? Did he answer?'

As if sensing Avni's predicament, Rithik answered those unasked questions. 'I know why you asked that question. An underwear is one's own dirty little secret. You wanted to know if he cleaned his mess and not leave it behind for you to clean like many men in our society!'

Avni looked at Rithik with her mouth agape. That question came to her mind one day when her dad was angry for not having clean underwear to wear. It was then that she realised that while her mother and she regularly washed their own underwear, her father didn't. He relied on the servants or sometimes even on his wife for that. It was then that Avni started looking at the world from a different perspective. It was then that she noticed that the men in her family treated the women as servants. Upscale and high maintenance, but servants. The vast difference between a wife and a servant was blurred and merged into one.

'Avni?' Rithik snapped in front of her.

Avni came back to her senses and said, 'I am sorry. I was

thinking about something.'

Rithik had come here with a plan. He wanted to ask Avni out on a date. But on seeing the heart-shaped mark, he had completely forgotten about his plan. 'Avni, I really like you!' he said, taking her hand in his. 'Would you like to go out on a date with me?'

'Did… are…'

'I want to know the Avni who created the page Prashasti, not the Avni who lived in the Karamsheel house,' said Rithik, rubbing his thumb against her birthmark.

'I…' Avni wanted to say yes. But she was afraid. Afraid that this relationship would also be doomed like her relationship with her parents.

'There is no rush. I mean, I just wanted to make my intentions clear. I like you. And now the ball is in your court.' Rithik grabbed the notepad and pen from the centre table and scribbled something, 'This is my phone number. If you wish to talk, please do. I would be more than happy to listen to you.' And just like that, impressing Avni, Rithik left.

'You fool, go say yes!' Tanvi said, coming out from her hiding spot.

'Tanu…'

'Avni, you said you liked him. You won't stop talking about him ever since you left the house. There is something between you two. It needs to be explored and can only be done if you two date and spend some time together!'

When Tanvi's word sank in Avni, she dashed for the gates while behind her she could hear Tanvi chuckling. Avni had lost enough of her time living in fear, but not anymore.

'Rithik!' Rithik heard her behind him. He knew it was Avni. He just hoped that she hadn't come out to reject him. When he turned around, he saw her flustered and gasping for air. Did she run all the way here? Why?

'I would like to go out on a date with you!'

10

Do You Love Me?

Days passed by and with each passing day, Avni felt happy, comfortable, and cherished with Rithik and his family. Not once did they make her feel as if she wasn't a part of the family. Kusum Aunty was always willing to listen to her. Krishna Uncle was always there to guide her. Rithik… Rithik made her feel so loved and cared which she had never felt in her life, ever.

With each passing day, Rithik grew restless. He had long ago known that he wanted to be by Avni's side, but now, there was this fear that had started creeping up in his mind. The fear of losing her. The fear of not being enough for her. He knew that in the end, he would never force his decision on Avni. But a primitive part of him wanted to take her away, to some land unknown, where it would just be the two of them.

Avni had a new question in her mind which she knew that only Rithik could answer. But she was uncertain, sceptical, and not sure as to how she should approach Rithik with that question.

'What's got that worried look on your face?' Tanvi asked from the doorway.

'Tanu, I… it's been almost a month since I started dating Rithik. I have known him before this whole dating thing started between the two of us. I liked him before, but now, I feel different. As if… if I don't see him or talk to him, then I won't find peace!'

Smiling, Tanvi joined her friend on the bed. 'It feels different. The satisfaction that comes after you eat your favourite dessert, *jalebi*. The perfection that you crave in your dishes!'

'It's more than that, Tanu. He is like salt in my cake. I am everything more when I am with him. Just like when you add salt to the cake, it adds more to the flavour of the cake,' explained Avni to her best friend.

Tanvi smiled up at her best friend. She understood what she was going through. Any person with eyes could tell that Avni was in love with Rithik, but she had yet to come to terms with that fact. 'I think you should talk to Rithik.'

Resting against the headboard, Avni sighed, 'A part of me doesn't want to tell him anything because that might inflate his ego. Another part wants to go on the rooftops and scream out my love for him…'

'Did you…' gasped Tanvi, 'You said…'

'I didn't say anything,' said Avni getting down from the bed.

'Avni, I think even Rithik loves you!'

'How can you say that?' grumbled Avni.

Tanvi shrugged, 'I just have a hunch.'

Snapping her fingers, Tanvi said, 'You know what, I have an idea. I know exactly how to make Rithik confess!'

Dear Rithik,

I think I am in love with someone. Should I tell him? Would he take well to the news? Should I make some grand gesture? What could be the best possible way to confess?

@prashasti

'What are you doing?' Avni took back Tanvi's phone.

Tanvi arched her eyebrows, 'Do you have a better plan?'

She shook her head.

'Great, then we are doing this. This way, you won't be backing out. Otherwise, I know you. You would keep stalling. This is the best way to get the truth out in the open!'

Avni might not have a better plan but she kind of knew that Rithik might not like this. He was a private person.

'Tanu, wait!' called out Avni.

But by then, Tanvi had pressed the send button. Tanvi looked back at her friend in horror. Then her phone pinged with an Instagram message alert. Rithik not only got the message. He had also replied.

Dear Prashasti,

I am happy that you are in love with someone. You should definitely tell him. He will surely take well to the news. Telling someone that you love them is a grand gesture in itself. The best possible way to confess is certainly not on Instagram. But I am happy that you did.

I love you too, Avni Prashasti Karamsheel.

Dr Rithik D. Kashyap
@yourmarriageguide

'What does it say?' Avni asked nervously.

'That he loves you too,' came Rithik's voice behind her.

'Rithik…' breathed out Avni.

'I love you, Avni. You are my prayers answered,' Rithik confessed, taking her in his arms.

Looking up into his eyes, Avni asked, 'How did you get in?'

Both Rithik and Tanvi cracked up at that. Trust Avni to not get to the point.

'Did you forget, my dear best friend, that you gave him the codes to the locks on the door one night?' prompted Tanvi. With that, Tanvi exited the room, closing the door behind her.

'Tell me,' urged Rithik.

'I love you, Rithik.'

*****

Avni and Rithik were standing outside Rithik's house.

'Everything is going to be fine,' Rithik assured Avni for the hundredth time.

They were at Rithik's house for dinner. While in the past, Avni never had an issue with it. Today, she was nervous as hell. For today, they were going to tell Rithik's parents about their love. She was worried about his parents' reaction.

Taking her hand into his, Rithik again reassured Avni, 'It will be fine. Let me tell them.'

Gently squeezing her hand, Rithik asked, 'Ready?'

'Yes,' nodded Avni.

Rithik pressed the doorbell.

Kusum had seen her son along with Avni standing on the porch for the past ten minutes. She had almost opened the door when her son finally rang the doorbell, and Kusum immediately dashed for the door.

'Avni!' said Kusum, pulling her into a hug.

'Ma!' grimaced Rithik.

Kusum shushed him.

'Ma, we have something important to tell you. Can we come in?' scowled Rithik.

What could he possibly have to say now? Kusum hoped that they weren't breaking up. It wasn't until she released Avni from her embrace that Kusum noticed the joined hands of her son and Avni. Guaranteed that they had told her and Krishna about their dating but never had she seen them hold hands like that, at least not when they were in this house, what could it mean? Kusum's eyes lit up at the possibility of Rithik and Avni's marriage. 'Yes, let's go in!'

They were all seated around the dinner table. Rithik pulled Avni's hand into his under the table. He mouthed it will be fine.

'So, what is it that you wanted to tell us?' Krishna asked between the bites.

'Avni and I are in love with each other.' Rithik ripped it off like a band-aid.

The spoon fell from Kusum's hand and clattered on the plate. Krishna started coughing furiously.

Rithik and Avni weren't sure what to make out of the parents' reaction.

'Oh, my God! My babies are in love!' jumped up Kusum. She went around the table to hug both Rithik and Avni.

'Just a month was enough. Wasn't it?' Krishna smirked at his son.

'Yeah,' grinned Rithik.

After dinner, Rithik and Avni walked hand in hand towards the car. On reaching the car, Rithik unlocked it and pulled up the passenger side door for Avni. He jogged around and climbed into his seat, clicked his seat belt glanced over to ensure that Avni had her seat belt on.

Rithik started the car. 'I think that went okay!'

A smile split over Avni's face, 'More than okay!'

'Yeah!'

'I love you, Rithik!' she said and Rithik's face split into a wide grin.

'I love you, too!'

On reaching her house, Avni jumped out of the car.

'Don't ever jump out like that. Wait for me to come around!' fumed Rithik.

'Being chivalrous, are we?' joked Avni.

'Yes!' replied Rithik pulling her into his arms.

Rithik didn't want to part with Avni, not yet. Not when this all still felt surreal. 'Can I stay the night?' he blurted out.

But then he realised that he shouldn't have rushed like this. 'I… I am sorry. It's just that this all feels surreal. I…' Avni placed her lips on Rithik's before he could utter another word. It wasn't exactly a kiss. Hell, it wasn't even a peck. It was barely a brush of her lips on his. But the intensity that both of them felt was enough to burn holes through the walls.

Avni ran back inside the house after that brush of lips, her breath laboured, cheeks flustered, heartbeat erratic. Standing against the door, Avni tried to calm herself by taking deep breaths. But it was futile because Rithik had followed her and not gone back to his home like Avni expected.

'You didn't answer my question,' said Rithik hoarsely.

Avni bobbed her head.

Rithik felt a weight lift off his heart when he saw Avni's nod. 'Just so you know I want to hold you tonight and nothing else. You still feel like a dream to me, Avni. Will you let me hold you tonight? Will you sleep in my arms tonight?' Rithik whispered in Avni's ear.

How could Avni say no to such a simple request? And that was only what they did that night, sleep in each other's arms. Guaranteed, that it was uncomfortable for Rithik to sleep in his jeans, but it was all worth it because Avni was still in his arms when he woke up the next morning.

Epilogue

Six months later

You are the salt to my cake,
Chocolate sauce to my vanilla ice cream.

Rithik read the message on his phone. He liked how Avni always chose to compare him and his love towards her to something minimalist yet important. For that was exactly how it was. They both had some admirable qualities which when combined created something more, an exceptional quality. Just like the cake and the vanilla ice cream. They both tasted good without salt and chocolate sauce but together it enhanced the flavour.

Rithik was still grinning like a lunatic when Tanvi barged into his office. 'You!'

'Tanvi?' Rithik was surprised to find her in his office. Behind him, he saw his assistant had followed her.

'I am sorry, sir. But she…' mumbled the assistant.

'It's okay. I will talk to her. She is a friend. You may go,' Rithik told the assistant.

The assistant was almost at the door when Tanvi called out, 'Close the door behind you. Will you?'

Once the two of them were alone, only then did Rithik ask her, 'How may I help you today, Tanvi?'

Tanvi leisurely moved towards the chairs opposite Rithik and sat down very gracefully in one of them. Rithik was puzzled; a moment ago, she was almost going to kill him and now she was… well she was acting very regally.

Clearing her throat, Tanvi began, 'I would like to know what your intentions with my best friend are.' She gazed at him seriously, yet with a pinch of mischief in her eyes.

Rithik wanted to laugh at this absurd situation, but he felt it wouldn't be the right thing to do. Who knew, Tanvi might switch back into her banshee mode.

Settling back in his seat Rithik replied, 'You know of my intentions, Tanvi!'

'No, I don't,' snapped back Tanvi.

'You know I love her,' tossed Rithik.

'Love isn't enough. Are you ever going to make an honest woman out of her?' declared Tanvi.

Rithik wanted to laugh so badly. He had to bite the insides of his cheek to control his laughter. Here was a best friend asking to make an honest woman out of her best friend. And she was doing it with utmost grace. He had imagined this moment with Kadam Karamsheel, but that man was pathetic. Rithik had yet to tell Avni about his meeting with her parents. He wondered if she would get mad.

Tanvi snapped her fingers, 'Seriously, Rithik. You are zoning out now!'

'I am sorry.'

Tanvi arched her eyebrows. Being the best friend, Tanvi

considered it her duty to ask about Rithik's intentions; after all, Avni's parents weren't going to ask. She drummed her fingers on the desk, waiting for Rithik to add more.

Finally, Rithik pulled out something from his desk drawer. Was that what Tanvi assumed it to be? It looked like a ring box. But not presuming things, Tanvi looked up at Rithik. He simply nodded.

'My intentions have been clear from Day One, Tanvi. I want to marry your best friend and grow old together.' Tanvi's eyes brimmed with tears at that confession. 'Then why the hell you haven't asked her yet? It has been six months!' sobbed Tanvi.

Passing out a tissue to Tanvi, Rithik said, 'Rest assured, I won't delay any further,' which earned Rithik a grin.

'Do you want me to help you in any way?' Tanvi asked excitedly.

'I think I have it under control.'

'You better hurry,' warned Tanvi getting up from her seat.

Today, he would ask Avni. Yes, it had to be today.

*****

Rithik was in his bathroom, applying cologne when his phone chimed.

I need you here, right now!

It was Tanvi. Something was wrong, seriously wrong. Rithik could feel it. He immediately grabbed his car keys and made his way down to the garage.

When he reached Tanvi's house, he was shocked to see the gates open. The girls had always been protective of their security. He silently went inside the house, but nothing seemed out of place. But then, he suddenly heard a sob. Rithik's skin prickled; he knew it was Avni. She was the one sobbing, but why? He hurried towards her room.

Tanvi was thankful that Rithik came here in record time. If anyone could calm Avni right now, then it was Rithik. Tanvi saw the pained look on his face and ushered Rithik to come near. As if sensing his presence, Avni freed herself from Tanvi's embrace and jumped into Rithik's arms.

'Shh… shh, love,' Rithik stroked Avni's back.

'Ma…' sobbed Avni.

Rithik pulled her out of his embrace and wiped her tears. 'Shh… it's okay. We will work it out, together. Whatever it is.'

Tanvi handed Avni a glass of water. Avni very slowly tried to gulp the water. When done, she again wanted to cry at the injustices done to her mother. But then, she felt Rithik squeeze her hand. She looked up into his eyes and only found love. It gave her strength. After taking a few deep breaths, she finally told them the whole story. The unfair life that her mother was living.

'I never knew any of this. She never told me. When she told me all of it today. Things finally started to click in my mind. I wasn't a good daughter. I left her alone with that vile man,' Avni's eyes brimmed with tears.

Tanvi pulled her friend in a hug. 'It's okay. Let it out,' Avni silently sobbed on Tanvi's shoulder.

'I don't know what to do, Tanu. How to help her?' whispered Avni.

'Babe, we will find a way out,' Tanvi assured her.

Rithik was still horrified to learn about the pain and torture Sandhya Karamsheel went through. He needed to act fast. There was still hope that Sandhya might fight back and heal into a happy person. Rithik aimed to achieve that. His profession demanded that he helped Sandhya, and he would. He suddenly remembered the day when he met the Karamsheels. 'In light of recent events, I have a confession to make, Avni.'

Avni furrowed her brows. 'What is it?'

'Some days back, I went to meet your parents. I had hoped that they might see some sense. I might persuade them. But it was all in vain. Your mother…' he took Avni's hand in his, 'I think you might have inspired your mother. I think knowing that her daughter is happy might have pushed her to find her own happiness. I think she came here today to see for herself if it was all true. She might have come seeking help or to draw more inspiration from you!'

'I… you really think so?'

'Yes!'

'Can we help her?'

'Yes.' Rithik cupped her cheek with another hand.

'Thank you!'

*****

A few months later

Avni hugged Rithik. They had won. They had finally managed to get justice for her mother. 'Thank you!' she kissed Rithik's cheek.

Rithik was glad that it was all finally over. No one deserved a life full of torture. Yes, it was hard to show Sandhya that she was living a harmful life. But in the end, she understood. And now, Rithik prayed for happiness and only happiness in her life ahead.

Rithik was dropping them all—Avni, her mother, and Tanvi—back home. Avni and her mother were walking ahead hand in hand. They looked happy. Avni was happy that she got her mother back.

'You know, you deserve your own happiness,' said Tanvi, coming beside him.

He simply nodded.

'You were going to propose to her that night, weren't you?'

He again nodded. There was no sense in hiding it.

Jutting her chin, Tanvi said, 'You should do it tonight. Make it more special!'

'I don't think so,' chuckled Rithik.

'I am serious, Rithik.'

'She needs time.'

'She doesn't. What has she always told you? You are the chocolate sauce to her vanilla ice cream. You only bring more into her life.' With that, Tanvi jogged up and joined the ladies ahead.

Rithik was stunned. Tanvi's words made sense. But the question was, could he really do it tonight?

Yes, he could.

Rithik spotted Avni on the sofa sitting between her mother and best friend. He pulled her up.

'Rithik,' she whispered, all flustered.

'I will give you a few hours with your mother and best friend. Then I am coming back for you!'

Sandhya's eyes glistened with unshed tears. She never would have imagined that she would start her life again at the age of forty-eight. But her daughter, her beautiful Avni, had inspired her. And Rithik encouraged her, guided her. It was amazing. She was learning to walk, and her daughter was helping her. She had never helped Avni with any of her firsts; she wasn't the one to help her daughter take her first steps. But her daughter, she had resilience. It was funny that a meek woman like herself had given birth to such a resilient woman like Avni.

Rithik left. Avni stared at his retreating back. She had so many things to tell him. In the past few months, she wasn't sure that she had ever told him that she loved him but still, he was there, always. He always had her back. Avni hugged herself, thinking how lucky she was to have a man like Rithik in her life.

'You know, I am jealous that you got a man like Rithik in your life,' remarked Tanvi. 'Don't you want to make an honest man out of him?' Tanvi thought that if the line had worked on Rithik, then it would surely work on Avni.

Sandhya's eyes lit up at Tanvi's suggestion. The idea of seeing her daughter married off and that too to a man she loved was a pleasant thought.

Avni turned around to face her best friend, 'Did you…' Avni's gaze switched to her mother, who had a similar expression as Tanvi. Did they really suggest what she thought they suggested?

'I think it's high time that you both got married,' shrugged Tanvi. Avni's mother was bobbing her head enthusiastically beside her friend. They were serious. Avni tried to picture her life as a married woman.

'I think I need proposal ideas,' declared Avni.

Tanvi jumped up and hugged her best friend. This was it. 'I have plenty!' She exclaimed.

Chuckling, Avni replied, 'Of course, you do!'

Meanwhile, in the other corner of the city, Rithik was all set to make his way back to Avni.

'Are you going to propose tonight?' his mother asked from the doorway. His father was also there.

'I think so,' he replied, flipping the ring box open for Kusum to see.

'You *think* so? Son, you need to be sure. This is a life-long decision. A commitment you are going to make!' commented his father.

'I am sure, Dad. Maybe a little nervous.'

Kusum hugged her son. She had waited a long time for this day. She was happy to see Avni and his love blossom into something life-long. 'I am proud of you. All the best!' she kissed his cheek.

Krishna hugged his son and backslapped him. 'Now, go, and don't mess up,' he chortled.

Rithik chuckled at his parents, 'Thanks, you guys. You are the best. I love you!' He rushed out of his room.

Kusum and Krishna watched their son rush through the gates. They had tears in their eyes, but they were happy. Their son was in love. What parents wouldn't be happy?

Rithik pressed the doorbell.

'Hi!' Avni's voice came from behind him. What was she doing out here? Before he could ask her, she started pulling his hand. 'Come!'

Avni was nervously excited to do this. She moved or at least tried to move with utmost grace up the stairs. Never did she leave Rithik's hand.

Behind her, Rithik very anxiously asked Avni, 'Where are we going?'

'You will see!'

Finally, they were up on the terrace. Rithik was surprised to see the whole terrace. It was lit up and decorated.

'Are we celebrating something?' prompted Rithik.

Avni ignored his question and took his other hand in hers.

Grabbing onto both of his hands, Avni forced him to look into her eyes.

'Rithik, there might be some cosmic connection between us, because no way in hell do I deserve you.' Rithik wanted to argue but Avni put her elegant finger on his lips. 'Shh... let me finish.' Rithik nodded for her to continue.

'I don't know whether what's between us is love or something else. I only know that when I am with you, I am more, and I don't want to miss being more. Call me greedy, but I want that more, that outstanding me. With you, I can be selfish, happy, cranky, and at peace. I want it all, always!' Avni immediately dropped down to her knees.

'Dr Rithik Dhananjay Kashyap, I have one very important question to ask you,' Avni presented Rithik with a ring. 'Will you marry me?'

Smiling, Rithik too got down on his knees. 'Avni Prashasti Karamsheel, you are my prayers answered. As for your very important question, I was supposed to ask that particular question.' Rithik took out his ring from his jeans pocket, 'Will you marry me?'

Avni looked at Rithik and then back at the ring in his hand. 'I asked you first!'

Tanvi and Sandhya giggled from their hiding spot. Tanvi had insisted on being present to record the whole proposal and Avni had liked the idea, so she readily agreed. Avni's mother had simply accompanied Tanvi.

Rithik too chuckled at Avni. 'That you did, love.' He gently brushed his lips over hers. 'Yes. Yes, I will marry you!'

Avni jumped into Rithik's arms. They both fell back to the ground, 'Yes, I will marry you!' whispered Avni in Rithik's ear.

Kusum and Krishna had also joined them by now. Kusum

laughed at seeing her son so happy. Avni finally remembered that they had company. For a moment, she had even forgotten about Tanvi and her mother. She immediately got up from the ground and gave Rithik her hand.

*****

It took another two months for Avni and Rithik to finally marry but it was worth the wait. Within those two months, they thoroughly enjoyed being engaged. The social media and the news agencies went crazy when they got hold of Rithik and Avni's love story. Millions of single girls' hearts broke when they learned that their famous marriage therapist was getting married and that too to a food blogger. Some fans even pointed out that they were meant to be together, one just had to look at their names. Rithik and Avni didn't understand what they meant by that. But another fan later clarified that while Rithik's full name was Dr Rithik Dhananjay Kashyap, Dhananjay which was also another name for Arjun from Mahabharata. Avni's full name was Avni Prashasti Karamsheel. In some folklore, Draupadi from Mahabharata was also known as Prashasti. Rithik and Avni were speechless at this revelation. They were just thankful that something had led them here, at this point, in each other's arms.

~ The End ~

Would you consider

leaving a review?

Author's Biography

Shristi G, a young girl from a small town, fostered a deep passion for literature from an early age. With an insatiable appetite for reading, she found solace in books. However, it was during the COVID-19 pandemic that she embarked on a journey to craft a truly memorable character. Inspired by this experience, Shristi now aspires to bring forth a multitude of remarkable characters in her future endeavours.

We love creating beautiful books for you!

Come be a part of our ever-growing community of authors. Grow, write, and publish with us!

Scan here to explore books, authors and more

Connect with us on socials. We'd love to hear from you!

    Inkfeathers Publishing